If Jesus Lived In My Neighborhood

By Nate, Amya & Alana Bull

Acknowledgements

Nate, Amya and Alana are part of the Urban Apostolic Network Church (UANC), which you can find out more about at www.urbanapostolic.org. They would like to thank the Explorers class at Centerpoint Church, their friends John and Pat, the Hosack family, Jackie Folkert, Sandy Wolfinbarger and many more. If you love the book please buy many more for you friends! Our desire is that families would read this together and find trust in Jesus through it.

In Christ,

Nate, Amya and Alana

About This Book

"When Jesus heard that John had been put in prison, he withdrew to Galilee. Leaving Nazareth, he went and lived in Capernaum, which was by the lake in the area of Zebulun and Naphtali." – Matthew 4:12-13

"A few days later, when Jesus again entered Capernaum, the people heard that he had come home. They gathered in such large numbers that there was no room left, not even outside the door, and he preached the word to them." – Mark 2:1-2

I like to walk and pray. Something about walking and feeling the outdoors flow through my lungs really helps me connect with the Lord. I especially like doing strolls, the kind of meandering that barely even gets your heart rate up. Ideally, these excursions take place with very little sunlight. This means that I'm often ambling along one of the side streets in my neighborhood at four a.m. or eleven p.m. listening for direction from the Almighty.

Sometimes it gets switched up on me. On one such occasion, instead of early in the morning or late at night, I was walking along on a sun-filled, crisp afternoon. It must have been a weekday because there was very little activity on the street. As I was enjoying moments alone with the Lord, the Holy Spirit whispered into my heart, "What if Jesus lived in that house right there?"

I paused and waited for more.

More never came.

I looked at the nearest house. There wasn't anything overwhelming about it. It was a nice home, but I was failing to see why the Holy Spirit mentioned it at all. Eventually I continued with my stroll, but the idea stuck in my head. What if Jesus lived in my neighborhood?

A few days later, I was reading in Matthew when I ran across the verse in chapter four. As with many familiar passages, I was tempted to just skim-read it until the words almost jumped off the page for me. It was almost like I was reading it for the first time. Matthew 4:12-13 says, "When Jesus heard that John had been put in prison, he withdrew to Galilee. Leaving Nazareth, he went and lived in Capernaum, which was by the lake in the area of Zebulun and Naphtali."

Wow! Do you see it?

Capernaum is north of Nazareth where Jesus lived with his parents. According to this scripture, it appears that some time after the beheading of John the Baptist, Jesus moved from Nazareth to Capernaum. This was a weird thing for me to think about. Some of it had to do with something I had internalized about the meaning of Luke 9:58 where Jesus says, "Foxes have dens and birds have nests, but the Son of Man has no place to lay his head." I took this to be literal without considering that, in the context of the verse, it has other meanings.

If you look carefully at that passage in Luke 9, Jesus says this in response to someone telling him that he would be a committed disciple. In response, Jesus expresses the thing about foxes and birds and nests and dens. He was pointing to the necessity of counting the cost of following him before just making a quick, rash decision. It's a decision that requires you to give up everything, including a right to comforts like a den or nest.

But this doesn't mean Jesus didn't have a home. Jesus did. It's right there in scripture. Mark 2:1 says, "A few days later, when Jesus again entered Capernaum, the people heard that he had come home. They gathered in such large numbers that there was no room left, not even outside the door, and he preached the word to them." And actually when the neighbors heard that he had come home, so many people rushed to the house that there wasn't even room outside the door. The very next verses tell us about a man who was paralyzed who needed healing. His friends, seeing that everyone had beat them to Jesus' house and that they couldn't even get to the door, dug through the roof. It never occurred to me that this was Jesus' roof. Wow! Isn't that amazing? Jesus had to do home repair!

So I began thinking about this idea: What would my neighborhood look like if Jesus lived in it? Then I got my two daughters, Amya and Alana, to brainstorm with me. We began to imagine together how different our neighborhood would be if Jesus lived right down the street. What would happen if, like what happened to the people who lived in Capernaum, one day a man named Yeshua moved in down the street. How would we first encounter him? What would our first impression of him be? At what point would we start to think he was something more than just ordinary? Would we be surprised at who he knew? Would we be surprised at who he hung out with? Would we be surprised at who hated him? Would we be surprised at who loved him?

As we continued with our imagination exercise, we began to write ideas down. Because we are all in love with Calvin and Hobbes, we began to draw out some of our ideas. It became apparent early on that this was something more than just a children's book. It's a case for the incarnational ministry that every believer is called to. Selah.

But it's also more than that.

This is an invitation to allow your mind to begin to imagine with us how different your neighborhood, job, school, church, etc. would be if Jesus was a part of it. And in the end, because of the overwhelming evidence in scriptures, we are making the case that Jesus *IS* a part of it. But I digress. I'm getting ahead of myself.

Please realize that this is completely fiction. But it's not really fiction at all. Some of the things that we included are purely from our wild imaginations. We included these ideas because it's fun. Some of the things we included are actually very tied to scriptural references. Where possible we are footnoting these scriptures so that the adult in you can go look it up and re-imagine a 21st-century Jesus.

Lastly, have fun! Our hope is that you can read this together as a family. One of my seminary professors told me that at the beginning level of teaching the Word of

God, my professors should be able to understand me. At the intermediate level of being able to teach the Word of God my congregation should be able to understand me. But the graduate level of being able to teach the Word of God, when someone is really starting to become good at teaching Biblical principles and truths, even children should be able to understand. Therefore we hope that, as simple as some of the ideas are, they will spark a conversation at the dinner table that will lead to real thought and faith.

Our hope is that you feel the freedom to color the pictures in. One of the reasons that we didn't color in any of the pictures is because we love to color. Hopefully you will take the opportunity to add to the book with your own artistic ideas in some way and in doing so become part of the process of seeing Jesus in your setting.

With Love,

Nate, Amya & Alana Bull

One day a new man moved into our neighborhood.[1] He moved into that small house near the end of the block. Mom said we should go bring him some of our world-famous potato soup to welcome him to the area. We thought we would after the next round of Mario Kart we will. We were all sick of our brother winning every time, and we figured the dude down the street could wait. He probably wanted some time to settle in anyway. Right?

_____

[1] Matthew 4:12-13; Mark 2:1-2; Isaiah 9:1-2

THINKING TOGETHER - 1

1.   Read Matthew 4:12-13 and Mark 2:1-2. What do you think the

     people living in Capernaum thought about Jesus when he moved

     into their neighborhood?

2.   How would your neighborhood look different if Jesus moved in

     next door?

After lunch we went down the street to introduce ourselves and bring

the new guy a care basket with the soup. When we got to the house,

we could hear someone whistling a tune. We knocked on the front door

and the man answered in just a few seconds. His smile was warm and

inviting. After introducing ourselves, he told us his name was Yeshua[2]

(although he said he could be called Yehoshua, Joshua or Josh as well if

any of those were easier). He invited us in while he finished cooking

lunch. I think he was cooking fish of some kind.[3] It smelled fantastic.

We probably shouldn't have gone into a stranger's house but, there was

something about this Josh. Something.....holy?

---

[2] Iésous is the Greek transliteration of Yeshua or Yehoshua which we pronounce "Jesus" in English. The name means "Savior" or "Jehovah Saves."
[3] John 21:9

THINKING TOGETHER - 2

Imagine meeting Jesus for the first time.

1.   What do you think you would like most about him?

2.   Do you think there would be anything that would surprise you

      about him?

3.   What do you think his house would look like?

4.   Would he have any pets? Would there be anyone living with

      him?

The house was way bigger on the inside than we thought was possible.

Joshua said he was preparing rooms for his brothers and sisters.[4] The

hallways were filled with hundreds and hundreds of pictures. We asked

Joshua who all the people were. He said these were his brothers and

sisters.[5] I thought it was impossible for anyone to have that many

brothers and sisters, but Josh could tell us each person's name, their

birthdays, and where they lived.[6] It got really interesting when we saw

a picture of "Ganny" our grandmother who had died a few years ago.

Joshua said he knew her very well and that they were really close

friends. We didn't know what to say. Who was this Yeshua?

---

[4] John 14:2
[5] Mark 3:35; Romans 8:17; 1 John 3:1
[6] Matthew 10:30; John 17:20-21

THINKING TOGETHER - 3

1.   Read John 14:2. What do you think Jesus means by this?

2.   Read John 17:20-21. When Jesus prays for you, what do you

think He prays about?

That night all we talked about was Joshua. He was so generous and kind. The fish he shared with us earlier that day tasted so good it seemed like a dream.[8] He was so fun to be with.[9] He laughed so hard when my sister spilled the Kool-Aid on his white carpet because he said the stain looked like someone he knew from Little Haiti. He wasn't even angry at all! None of us wanted to leave. We had spent the whole day with him.[10] The only reason we went home was so Mom wouldn't worry about us. We told her all about Josh. He told us we could come over whenever we wanted to. We all agreed to go back tomorrow as soon as we were done with breakfast. Here's something really weird: I think I already love Yeshua![11] I don't know why, but I know that I do.

---

[8] John 21:9
[9] Mark 12:37
[10] John 1:35-42
[11] Song of Solomon 1:4 (Message translation)

THINKING TOGETHER - 4

1. Read Mark 12:37. The New American Standard Version of the Bible translates this verse, "And the large crowd really enjoyed listening to him [Jesus]." What do you think would be so enjoyable about listening to Jesus?

2. Do you think Jesus would be angry if you spilled Kool-Aid on his white carpet? Why or why not?

As soon as we woke up the next morning we rushed downstairs to eat breakfast. We couldn't wait to see Josh again! Mom came into the kitchen to see why we were in such a hurry, and when we told her where we were getting ready to go, she told us we couldn't go over there. She said something about letting Yeshua get settled into his new house and not bothering him. We were so disappointed. We told her over and over again that Joshua had told us we could come over whenever we wanted to and after begging her for almost an hour she finally said yes. Mom did say we had to brush our teeth and clean our rooms first. We've never cleaned so fast! When we were done we sprinted over to Josh's house.[12]

---

[12] Mark 9:15, Mark 6:33, Matthew 19:1-2

THINKING TOGETHER - 5

1. If Jesus did live in your neighborhood, do you think you would

    be friends with him right away? Why or why not?

2. What do you think the inside of Jesus' house looks like?

When we finally got to Josh's house, he was eating breakfast with Jeremy and Daniel, two of our neighbors who get into a lot of trouble. We asked how they knew Yeshua. They said they met Josh at a party last night[13] and that he had healed their friend who was having a seizure.[14] "Healed? What do you mean by healed?" we asked. They said they were all dancing when their friend collapsed and went into convulsions. The party stopped and everyone was really scared. Someone called an ambulance and some people were even crying. Joshua knelt down and prayed for their friend who immediately calmed down and stopped shaking. In a few minutes, the friend sat up and was completely better.[15] Everyone was amazed! Jeremy and Daniel said they have been with Josh ever since and planned on following him anywhere he went.[16]

---

[13] John 2:1-2
[14] Mark 9:14-27
[15] Mark 9:14-27
[16] John 1:35-37, John 1:43

THINKING TOGETHER - 6

1. If Jesus did live in your neighborhood, who would be some of his

    good friends?

2. Can you think of a time you wish Jesus could have been with

    you so that he could have healed someone you know?

After Yeshua, Daniel, and Jeremy finished eating breakfast and doing the dishes, Yeshua asked if we wanted to walk to the park. He said he wanted to meet more people.[17] It didn't matter what we did as long as we did it with him. As we got near the park we saw some guys playing basketball. Actually when we got closer we saw one of the boys named Demari was in a lot of pain. I guess he had landed on his ankle wrong and broken it bad. Josh went over to him and helped Demari to his feet. His foot must have gotten "healed" just like Jeremy and Daniel's friend because Demari started walking around normally and testing his foot out. Sure enough, Josh had completely healed the foot. If we hadn't been there to see it we wouldn't have believed it. We're not even sure all of this is real.[18]

---

[17] Mark 1:38-39
[18] Mark 2:12

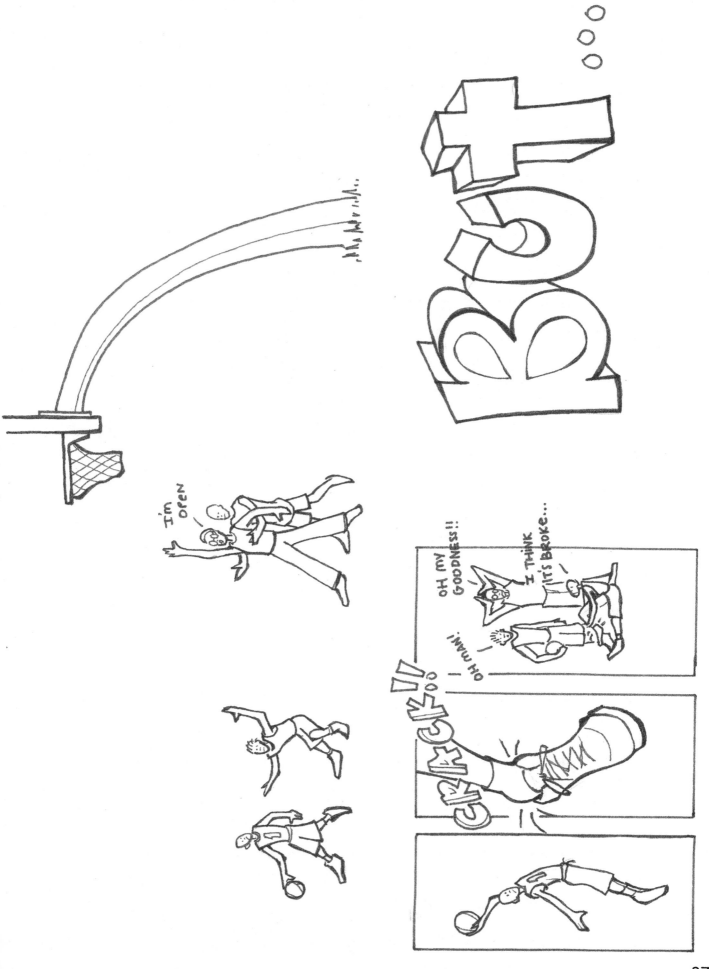

THERE WAS ABOUT TO BE A MEETING BETWEEN
YESHUA

THE CHANCE MEETING BETWEEN JOSH
AND THE YOUNG ATHLETE
WHO HURT
HIS ANKLE...

LET ME HELP YOU UP.

NEED OF ANY KIND

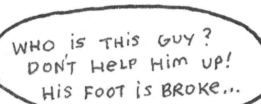
WHO is THIS GUY?
DON'T HELP HIM UP!
HIS FOOT is BROKE...

... WAS ABOUT TO SHOW, AGAIN, THE GLORY OF THE FATHER.

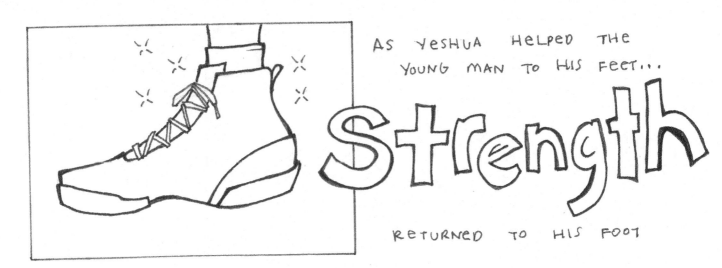

THINKING TOGETHER - 7

1.   Can you think of some reasons that Jesus would want to meet a

     lot of people?

2.   Read Mark 2:8-12. If you started walking around with Jesus

     everywhere, how would you start to change? How would your

     thinking change? How would your actions change?

We spent almost all day walking around with Josh. He seemed to love everyone we met.[19] It seemed like they loved him too. Instantly! We know what they are feeling. During our time with him, Joshua healed someone's back, he healed someone's toothache, he healed someone's shoulder, and did like at least a dozen other miracles.[20] Josh said the reason he could heal people was only because of his Father.[21] I guess his Father was working through Josh in some way? Joshua seemed to believe we could know the Father too.[22] Would this mean we would be able to help heal people like Josh did?[23] Finally, well after dinnertime was past, we went home. Mom and Dad yelled at us for an hour about worrying them by not telling them where we were. They said they were going to have a talk with this Yeshua about boundaries. We wished we never had to leave him.

---

[19] John 3:16
[20] Matthew 12:15-21
[21] John 5:30, John 14:10-11
[22] John 17:25-26
[23] John 14:12-14

THINKING TOGETHER - 8

1. Read John 5:30 and John 14:10-11. What do you think

    Jesus meant when He said, "By myself I can do nothing,"

    in John 5:30?

2. How do you think someone would get to know the Father?

The next day Mom walked with us to Josh's house. No one was home,

but there was a note taped to the door with our names on it. It said:

Dearest Friends,

I'm in the city of Zeeland for a few days. I have to preach there

at Gateway Community Church for a group of people I've known

for a long time. It's part of the reason I have come to this area.[24]

The door is open. Feel free to stay and eat some snacks if you

would like.

Yeshua

P.S. – Please tell your mom that you were with me all day

yesterday and that you're always safe with me ☺ I can't wait to

meet your parents!!!

How did he know my mom was worried?

_____

[24] Mark 1:35-39

THINKING TOGETHER - 9

1. Read Mark 1:35-39.

2. Why do you think Jesus wanted to preach in so many different cities?

3. What do you think happened in those cities after Jesus left?

My parents finally met Josh! We went to his house after dinner the other night and he was there with some of our neighbors. One of them, our little niece Laeyanna, was crying and Yeshua was talking to her. When Dad asked what was going on, we found out that Josh had just healed her from a skin disease[25] that was embarrassing to her because the other kids at her school teased her about it. Laeyanna was crying tears of joy! Dad and Mom got to talk with Joshua and now they like him just as much as we do.

---

[25] Matthew 8:1-4

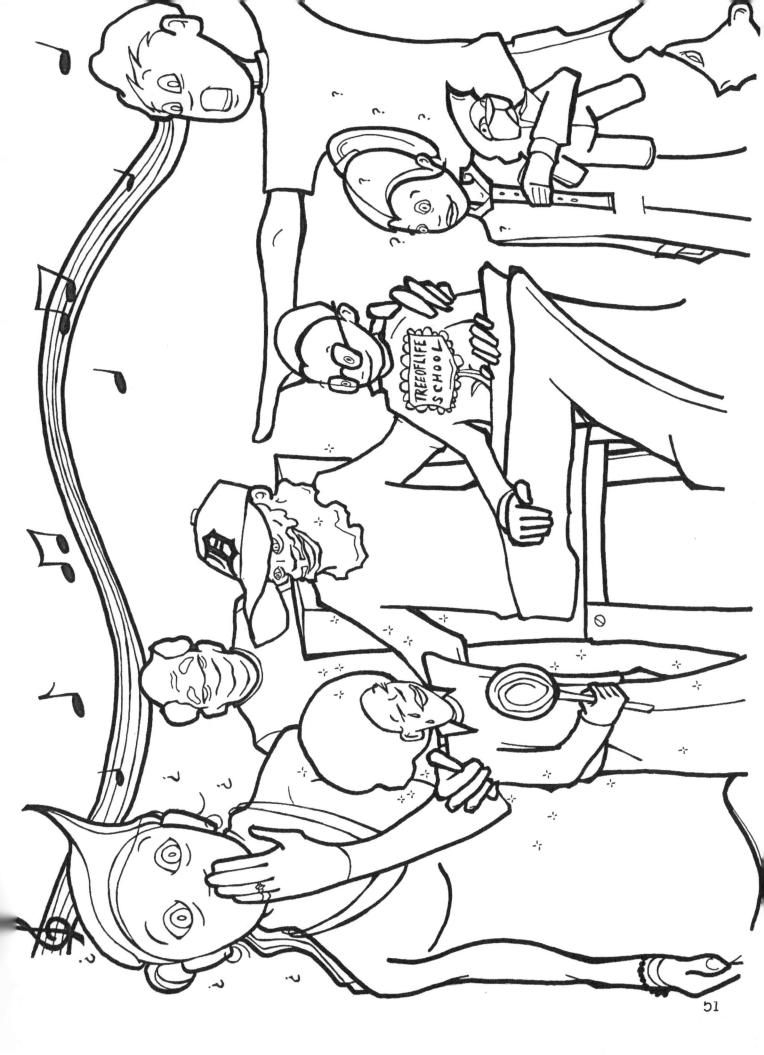

THINKING TOGETHER - 10

1. Read Matthew 8:1-4.

2. Do you think God really cares about a "little" thing like what our skin looks like? Why or why not?

3. What other "little" things do you think Jesus would heal?

A few weeks later, a lot of people started gathering around Josh's house. I guessed that meant he was probably home. We decided to go over there. Josh's house was packed.[26] There was even a news van out front. Most of our neighbors were there along with people of almost every color. Many of the people we had never seen before. It took us nearly ten minutes to push through the large group. We finally found him in the living room talking about the Father and something called the kingdom of Heaven?[27]

---

[26] Mark 2:2
[27] Matthew 13:31, Matthew 13:44

THIS IS ALANA STARR
REPORTING LIVE FROM
JUST OUTSIDE THE HOME
OF A MAN KNOWN
SIMPLY AS "YESHUA." AS
WE HAVE EARLIER REPORTED
THERE ARE ALLEGED
MIRACULOUS HEALINGS HAPPENING
HERE, AND BY ALL ACCOUNTS....

Mr. Sluiter, our next-door neighbor, was there talking with Josh. Mr. Sluiter had been unable to walk ever since his accident many years ago. Joshua whispered something to Mr. Sluiter and then helped him stand up. I almost fell over when Mr. Sluiter started walking right in front of my eyes. I didn't realize how tall he was! I'd never seen him standing before. Mr. Sluiter and his wife were weeping and jumping and praising the Father. The people in the room were also praising God.[28] I'm not sure why I was crying. It felt kind of like I'm at church when the singing is really good. Yeshua told all of us it was the presence of the Father. Then I knew I wanted to know the Father.

---

[28] Mark 2:12

THINKING TOGETHER - 11

1. Read Mark 2:1-12.

2. What do you think the man who got healed wanted to do first, now that he could walk?

3. What do you suppose people were thinking when they saw the miracle?

After that day, Yeshua couldn't go anywhere without large crowds following him. We heard he healed people everywhere he went. When he was in New York City, they had to shut down Times Square because of all the people trying to see him.[29]

---

[29] Mark 6:31

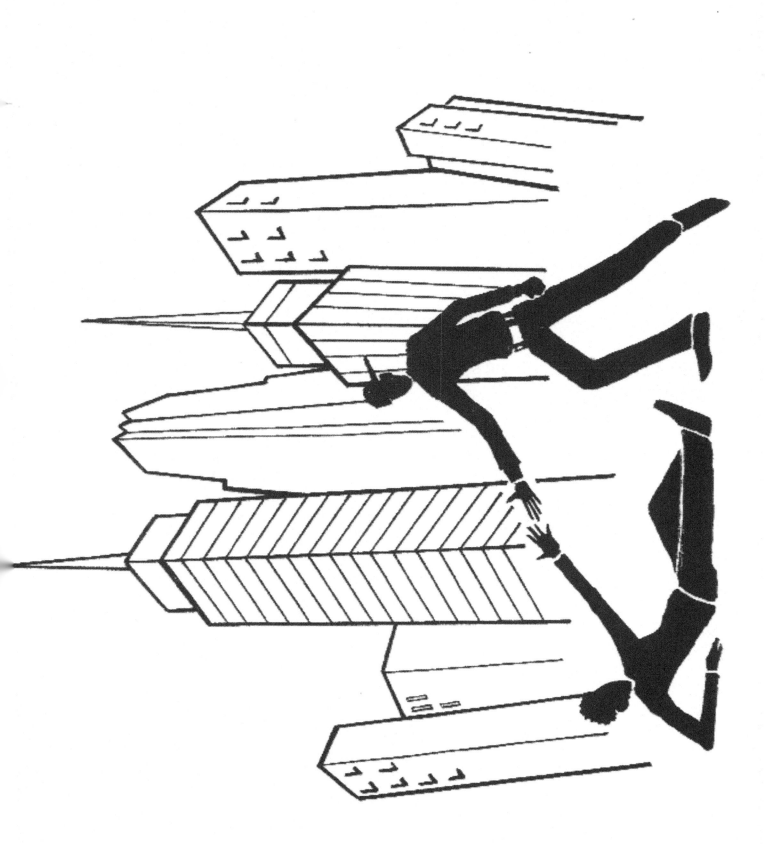

Everywhere Josh went he told people about the kingdom of Heaven and about the Father. I've seen people get so excited when they heard Joshua speak. I've even heard about people who have gotten healed just by hearing Josh talk. Josh says the Father is in love with us and can't wait to meet us.[30] If he's anything like Josh, I can't wait to meet the Father.

_____

[30] John 3:16, John 14:23

THINKING TOGETHER - 12

1.   Read Mark 1:14-15.

2.   What do you think Jesus is talking about when he tells people about the kingdom of God and the kingdom of Heaven?

3.   What won't be a part of the kingdom that God builds?

Everyone is talking about Josh. One of their questions is, "How does he know all these 'bad' people?" We know what they mean.

The other day when we were walking with Josh, we saw someone named Vernon. Joshua called out to Vernon and ran to meet him.

At first we were confused. We knew Vernon wasn't a good person at all

and that he had hurt people before. But that didn't stop Josh from

hugging Vernon tightly. I think Josh kissed him on the head??!!!

AT FIRST WE DIDN'T BELIEVE YESHUA COULD REALLY LOVE THAT MANY PEOPLE...

...BUT WE ARE STARTING TO BELIEVE IT NOW.

IT'S SOMETHING ABOUT THE WAY HE HUGS THEM.

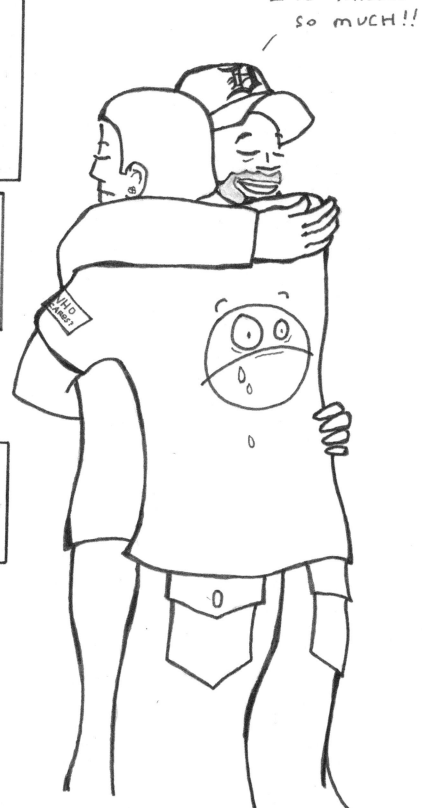

YOU CAN'T UNDERSTAND HOW MUCH I LOVE YOU. I'VE MISSED YOU SO MUCH!!

When we asked Josh why he would be friends with someone like Vernon, he told us the Father sent him to people just like Vernon. We asked Josh if he knew what kind of person Vernon was and Josh told us that he did. I guess they met the other day when Vernon was working for Ms. Dianne, and now Josh is going to be teaching Vernon about the Father every Friday.

THINKING TOGETHER - 13

1. Read Luke 7:33-35.

2. Now read Luke 19:1-10.

3. Why would Jesus want to be friends with "sinners?"

4. What do you think "sinners" liked about Jesus?

Today we heard that Josh caused a lot of trouble at the church down the street. I guess he got upset with some of the leaders there and some of the things they were doing. Anyway, he ended up smashing some things in their sanctuary and reminding them of certain Bible scriptures.[31] It doesn't sound like him at all! He is usually so kind. He must have been really, really, really upset about something. We can't wait to ask him why he was so upset.

---

[31] Luke 19:45-48; John 2:14-16

THINKING TOGETHER - 14

1. Read Luke 19:45.

2. Read John 2:13-22.

3. What do you think Jesus' disciples thought about his actions?

4. Would you still follow Jesus after he did something like this?

    Why or why not?

The leaders of the church where Yeshua caused trouble called a

meeting to talk about what he had done. Some said Joshua couldn't be

bad because of all the miracles he had performed.[32]

[32] John 3:2

Some said that no one who claimed to work for God would destroy stuff in a church. There was a lot of arguing. What's my opinion? If Josh was upset with them, there must be a good reason for it. We have seen too many things that prove to us that Josh is working for God.[33]

---

[33] John 10:38, John 14:11

THINKING TOGETHER - 15

1.   Read John 7:11-13.

2.   Why do you think the people were confused about who Jesus was?

3.   What would help you know if Jesus was a good man or a bad one?

4.   How do you think Jesus felt knowing some people liked him and some people didn't like him?

What would you say about someone like Yeshua?

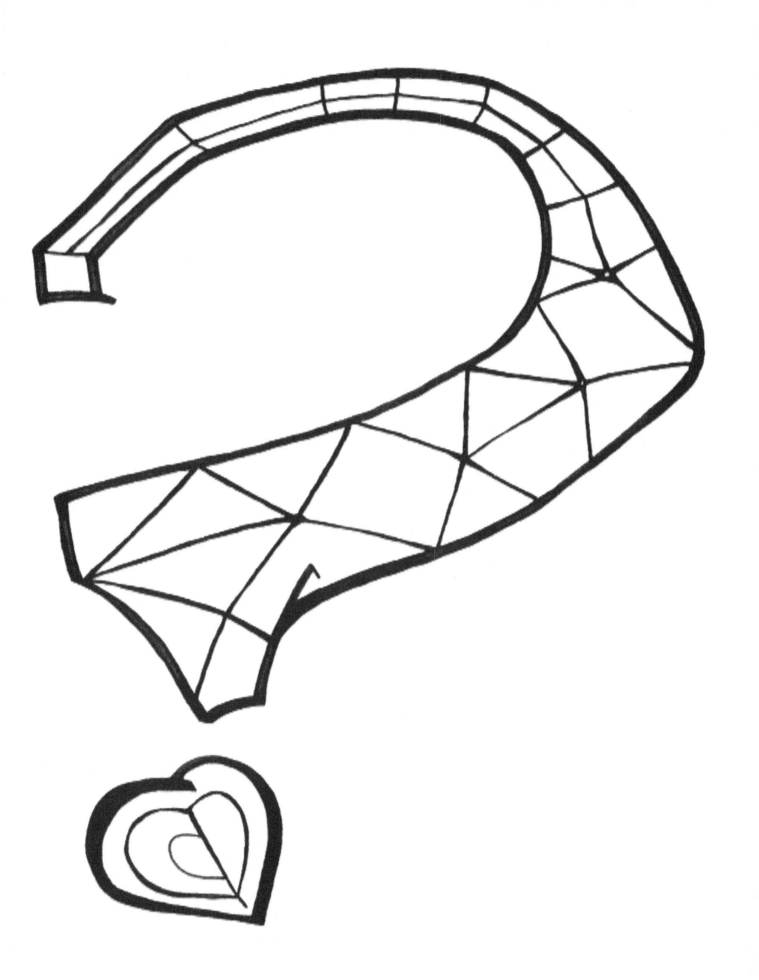

We saw him reading the Bible with his little nephew Darius...[34]

---

[34] Matthew 19:13-15

GOD SAW THAT THE LIGHT WAS GOOD

We saw Josh and his friends baptizing some people that they said were

becoming part of the family...[35]

―――――――――――――――――

[35] John 4:2, Acts 2:38-39

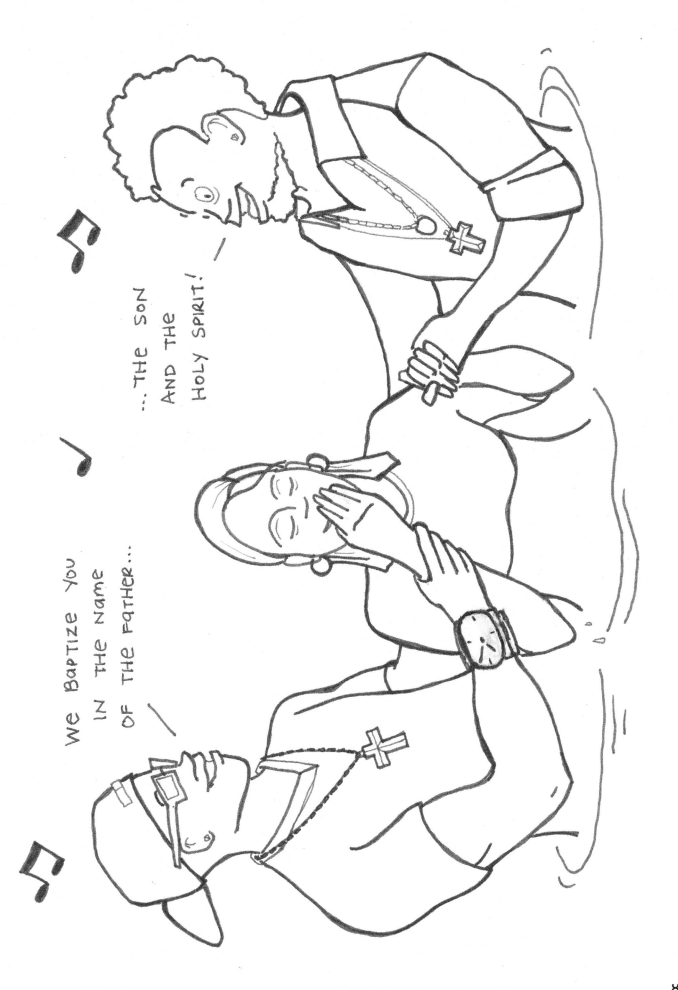

He was always praying and asking the Father for directions...[36]

_____

[36] Mark 1:35

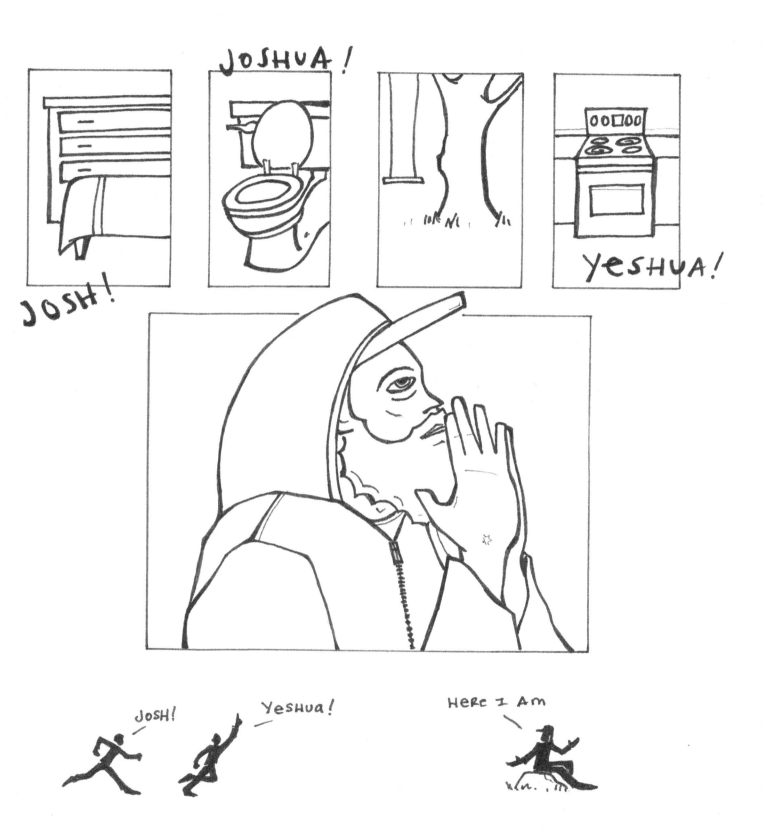

Yeshua even helped one of our friends named Esteven get free from

addiction. Apparently, Josh told some evil spirits to stop bothering

Esteven...[37]

---

[37] Luke 4:35, Matthew 17:18

...and now Esteven has changed so much some people call him Steve!

Does this sound like Josh is working for God?

THINKING TOGETHER - 16

1. Read John 3:16-17.

2. What did God give to save the whole world?

3. Why do you think God would heal people through Jesus?

4. Why do you suppose Jesus was always praying?

Yeshua is so much different than anyone else we have ever met!

Wouldn't it be amazing to have someone like that living in your

neighborhood? Well...

...JESUS DOES LIVE IN YOUR NEIGHBORHOOD!!!

Do you wanna know how?

THINKING TOGETHER - 17

1. Read Galatians 2:20.

2. Now read Colossians 1:24-27

3. What do these scriptures say about where Jesus the Son makes his home now?

4. If we believe this, how should we act in our neighborhood?

Lastly, please take some time to draw out what you think it would look

like if Jesus lived in your neighborhood!!

If Jesus Lived in My Neighborhood

If Jesus Lived in My Neighborhood

If Jesus Lived in My Neighborhood

Made in the USA
Middletown, DE
18 January 2019